What I Know for Sure
If I Change Nothing,
Nothing Will Ever Change

Ayin M. Adams, Ph.D.
Ciaara K. Carlsen

DELANE
PUBLISHING

Preface

What I Know for Sure: If I change nothing, nothing will ever change is literature written in a straightforwardly, readable format. This book is timely; as many are relying upon the old paradigms that no longer work. This book allows the reader to take a personal inventory, reflect, and review their own character.

Each page represents one of the 365 calendar days, whereby, thought-provoking queries, statements, and questions are put forth that force willing participants to become more responsible for their personal growth. On each of the pages, solutions are suggested. The ultimate realization is we are individually responsible for everything we think or do, the secret thoughts embedded in the recesses of our minds, or the physical actions that can be released like the swiftness of an arrow. The way in which we respond or do not respond to any situation is our own responsibility.

Dr. Adams and Ms. Carlsen assists readers in reevaluating their life experiences; directs them in being open to change; shares the necessity of adopting forgiveness into one's daily life; reminds those how receiving and trusting in the abundance of the Universe is always available; shares the importance of understanding the need to release fears so the ability to soar into ecstatic freedom can be realized.

The overused expression, *you are your worst enemy*, becomes a significant reminder of the importance of removing oneself from continued behavioral patterns that stifle the progress and block the flow thereby disallowing Change to take place.

Excuses, complaints and the blockages that prevent change require courage and a willingness to not continually repeat the same patterns. Dr. Adams and Ms. Carlsen solutions can prevent character stagnation, open the gates to more joy, and reduce pain if the work is done as a part of one's daily routine.

What I Know for Sure: If I Change Nothing, Nothing Will Ever Change provides a daily template for personal introspection and paves the way towards joy, clarity and self-improvement.

Gwyn Gorg; Author of *I Am the Blues*

Introduction

What I Know for Sure: If I Change Nothing, Nothing Will Ever Change, looks at change from a positive point of view. It requires an action and a commitment from the reader to engage in affirmative action in their life. What I Know for Sure realizes that most people moving through life resist change, thus the face to face confrontation, while examining conduct becoming, patterns, and behavior that demands a change in physical, mental, emotional, and spiritual transformation.

What I Know for Sure, confronts the reader to acknowledge choices made and choices not made while reflecting upon their experiences. The title commands attention of confidence and expecting change, while the tag line "If I Change Nothing, Nothing Will Ever Change demands an action to make different from what was.

On the pages of What I Know for Sure, you'll recognize fear, faith, and procrastination. Readers will understand what personal growth means, freedom to choose, and a deepening connection with the God of their own understanding. Trust will be a life-long companion on the pages of What I Know for Sure.

Co-author Ciaara K. Carlsen writes: "Choices for me were difficult because of lack of self-trust and fear of making the wrong decision. As I learn to listen to my inner voice and make choices and realize the good from the choices, I have begun to trust myself more."

Ms. Carlsen writes: "What I Know for Sure holds many

personal experiences especially during a time when I felt ready to make changes. I needed to go within to trust and have faith. As I made decisions it became apparent to me when I was on the right course because life flowed more easily, the right people appeared in my life (as if by magic) to help, and what I know for sure is there are no accidents in life."

Award-winning author, Dr. Ayin Adams writes in What I Know for Sure: "When I feel overwhelmed by situations and challenges in my life, I know that I must look at the choices I have made. I know that when I make choices that empower me, I am making choices from a place of love, trust, and joy…"

It is our hope and intention to inspire change by revealing that all knowledge we have lives within. There is never a wrong answer, just a choice and each choice we make is simply about what we need to learn at that moment, and not to fear because change is good, and change happens whether we like it or not.

May you learn to rely on what you know for sure, based on your life experiences as you continue to expand your relationship with yourself.

What I Know for Sure: If I Change Nothing, Nothing Will Ever Change, belongs in everyone's library.

Dr. Ayin Adams, Ph.D.
Ciaara K. Carlsen
November 11, 2018

Personal Assessment Inventory

Take this confidential assessment to help you create the change you want in your life. Remember, if you change nothing, nothing will ever change.

1. What extent do you depend on others?
2. In what ways do you depend on others?
3. How authentic are you?
4. Are you willing to stand on your principles?
5. Do you look before you leap?
6. How do you make your decisions?
7. Do you follow through on your decisions?
8. Are you self-confident, how?
9. Are you comfortable with trying new things?

After reviewing your thoughts, you should now have a clear idea of what it takes to be make changes for the better, stand in your own power, and live fully by being awake.

Taking the personal inventory below can help give you a better idea about where you are in life. As you begin to make change and become the change you want in your life, for each character defect, place a check in the space that you think best applies.

For example, if you disagree that you tend to rely on others to tell you what to do, say, or how to feel, then place a check in the "Disagree" space. On the other hand, if you think you have some aspects of that defect but not all of them, (such as that you think you often ask others too many questions that you can answer for yourself), then you can select "Somewhat Agree" in the space.

If I Change Nothing, Nothing Will Ever Change: Personal Assessment Inventory

	Disagree	Somewhat Agree	Agree
I tend to rely on others to tell me what to do, say, or how to feel.			
I tend to try to live through others.			
I tend to be intimidated by others and to cave to social pressures.			
I tend to keep to myself and avoid social interaction.			
I tend to sabotage my goals by intentionally trying to do the opposite of what others expect of me.			
I often feel as though I am playing a role instead of being the person I really am or want to be.			

It's like I'm a servant in our relationship, like what I want doesn't matter and what he/she wants does.

_____ _____ _____

I tend to do things that I know are wrong and feel guilty afterwards

_____ _____ _____

I tend to act impetuously or out of emotion without first considering the consequences and regret it later; or I become obsessed or anxious about making a mistake and have a hard time deciding.

_____ _____ _____

I often take alcohol or drugs to make myself feel better.

_____ _____ _____

I tend to put off following through on my decisions; or make excuses, or somehow get sidetracked and don't do what I intend to do.

_____ _____ _____

I often feel incompetent, stupid, or otherwise inadequate to make decisions for myself.

_____ _____ _____

I often try to please others
or get their approval in order
to validate my own self-worth. _____ _____ _____

I am afraid to try new
things. _____ _____ _____

The first step in making changes or improvements is make a personal commitment to change. It must be for yourself and not for others. You cannot afford to deceive yourself.

The second step in making changes or improvements is always to identify what needs to be changed or improved. Living a fully awake joy-filled life is pertinent to your growth and happiness. By identifying these things, it can be a first step in wakefulness.

The next step is the question: Where do you go from here?

The answer is to do your work. And this means to work with awareness, work cognitively, spiritually and emotionally on the character defects, short comings, and patterns you need to remove or transform. Getting professional help from a therapist or counselor can be useful, especially if you are feeling depressed or in desperation. You can then focus in on the defects you need most to work on. This book is devoted to creating change and living an authentic life.

What I Know for Sure

JANUARY

What I Know for Sure
If I change nothing, nothing will ever change

I, _____ make a commitment to myself this day _____ to change, to risk, to cry, to laugh, to be angry, to be in joy, to go through and grow through the challenges until I am standing steady and strong in my integrity and know that through change, I can overcome and know that anything is possible. I choose to commit now.

Reflections:

January 2 — What I Know for Sure

What I Know for Sure
If I change nothing, nothing will ever change

By remaining silent and allowing people to take advantage of me, I open the door for abuse. People can only exploit me when I allow them.

Reflections:

What I Know for Sure
If I change nothing, nothing will ever change

By moving through life daily, in the same way, among the same people, places, and things, life becomes stagnant. To change, I must consciously choose to explore life differently, which means letting go of what no longer serves me. If I change nothing, nothing will ever change.

Reflections:

January 4   What I Know for Sure

What I Know for Sure
If I change nothing, nothing will ever change

In times of anger or frustrations, we often say things or act in ways that create a void in relationships that wasn't there. People do not forget. This behavior diminishes our light. Once you say something, you can't take it back. Always watch your words or keep a watch on your mouth.

Reflections:

What I Know for Sure
If I change nothing, nothing will ever change

It is difficult to thrive when I choose to stay bound by chains of the past, limiting beliefs, family histories, and curses.

What I know for sure: living in my past, only brings my past into my present.

Time to let go!

Reflections:

What I Know for Sure
If I change nothing, nothing will ever change

Holding on to a thread of hope that my partner will one day come to my rescue. It is our long-distance relationship that keeps my hope alive. It's my turn now, even though my partner is emotionally, physically and psychologically unavailable.

Hope against hopelessness by holding onto a thread of hope.

Reflections: What relationships am I holding on to, even though I know that the person is unavailable, and the relationship is not serving my higher self? What were the warning signs and signals? Why did I ignore my gut feelings?

What I Know for Sure
If I change nothing, nothing will ever change

Some people don't like to be alone. They hear voices in their head and refuse to address the feelings. Being unavailable for self robs them of quality time and the privilege of introspection. Thoughts in their heads do not go away by surrounding self with people. The thoughts are still there, just temporarily quieted or ignored. I must like being alone with myself before I can expect others to be with me.

Today, I take time to be with myself.

Reflections:

What I Know for Sure
If I change nothing, nothing will ever change

What I know for sure: Spiritual messages received from God must remain for a period in incubation as I allow faith to take its course.

Reflections:

What I Know for Sure
If I change nothing, nothing will ever change

People have a hard time ending relationships or moving out of dire circumstances that offer no growth and development. They are reluctant to let go of the familiar and move into new areas of growth and unfoldment.

What I know for sure: it is easy to fall back into old patterns and behaviors, if I am not rooted and grounded in my truth.

Reflections:

What I Know for Sure
If I change nothing, nothing will ever change

Create time to slow down and listen.

What I know for sure: in my stillness, life's mysteries are revealed.

Reflections:

What I Know for Sure
If I change nothing, nothing will ever change

Life is always changing and evolving, I am open to stepping into change to experience the unknown.

Reflections:

January 12 What I Know for Sure

What I Know for Sure
If I change nothing, nothing will ever change

By moving through life daily, in the same way, among the same people, places, and things, life becomes stagnant. To change, I must consciously choose to explore life differently, which means letting go of what no longer serves me.

If I change nothing, nothing will ever change.

Reflections:

What I Know for Sure
If I change nothing, nothing will ever change

What I know for sure: when I feel afraid, I must ask myself is it real or is it:

False

Evidence

Appearing

Real

What I know for sure is that I am

Feeling

Excited

And

Ready

Reflections:

January 14   What I Know for Sure

What I Know for Sure
If I change nothing, nothing will ever change

What I know for sure: I choose the unknown to be my new normal.

Reflections:

What I Know for Sure
If I change nothing, nothing will ever change

During the birth of my child, a nurse stayed by my side, throughout labor and delivery providing strength and comfort that I desperately needed. Following the birth, she whispered in my ear softly, "it's time for me to go." "Will I see you tomorrow, I asked? "Yes," she replied. When I asked for her the next day, I was told there was no nurse by that name. Years later, I realized that it was my guardian angel sent to me by God.

What I know for sure: God does exist.

Reflections:

January 16 — What I Know for Sure

What I Know for Sure
If I change nothing, nothing will ever change

What I know for sure: when I surrender my concerns and put my trust in God, good things happen. I surrender my feelings to God and peace fills me.

Reflections:

What I Know for Sure
If I change nothing, nothing will ever change

What I know for sure: everything is in Divine Order, in spite of appearances.

Reflections:

January 18   What I Know for Sure

What I Know for Sure
If I change nothing, nothing will ever change

What I know for sure: I will not allow anyone to step on me. I am the door and not a door mat.

Reflections:

What I Know for Sure
If I change nothing, nothing will ever change

What I know for sure: life waits for no one. The time is now.

Reflections:

January 20   What I Know for Sure

What I Know for Sure
If I change nothing, nothing will ever change

If not now, when?

Reflections:

What I Know for Sure
If I change nothing, nothing will ever change

In the past, I've been lied to, manipulated, deceived, and abused. Despite the pain and heaviness in my heart, I am slowly releasing individuals who do not bring me joy and do not mean me well. And while this is not an easy decision, what I know for sure; this is the best way to be free from people whose negative energy can take me into dark places. My radiant self is to be in the light climbing higher up my spiritual ladder.

Reflections:

January 22   What I Know for Sure

What I Know for Sure
If I change nothing, nothing will ever change

What I know for sure: when I ask for help, I receive it.

Reflections:

What I Know for Sure
If I change nothing, nothing will ever change

What I know for sure: when I take responsibility for my life, I make internal changes for my growth and unfoldment, and the eternal changes are forever noted.

Reflections:

What I Know for Sure
If I change nothing, nothing will ever change

On Suffering: I must suffer to feel important.

If my experiences are not hard and I am not suffering enough, I sometimes think that my life does not count, because it is not painful, or there is no tragedy. This false belief tells me that I am not worthy. I must change my thinking to rid myself of this negative opinion and know that it is not the Will of God that I should suffer.

Reflections:

Ayin M. Adams, Ph.D. / Ciaara K. Carlsen **January 25**

What I Know for Sure
If I change nothing, nothing will ever change

Even challenges are gifts.
It's all in my perception.

Reflections:

What I Know for Sure
If I change nothing, nothing will ever change

My Spirit guides have appeared as strong women in my lineage to protect and guide me during difficult times, keeping me from harm. I acknowledge these courageous women: Lucille, Louise, Darlene, my daughter Cassedi, and myself.

Reflections: What strong women in your lineage do you acknowledge?

What I Know for Sure
If I change nothing, nothing will ever change

I often attract more of the same negative people or experiences until I pause and take time to find the lesson in the person or experience. What I know for sure, the challenges I have experienced in life are ways to measure my growth.

Reflections:

What I Know for Sure
If I change nothing, nothing will ever change

My past is not my future, each day is a new beginning and the past does not define what is happening now. The past can have no hold on me, unless I am allowing it or permitting it to be so.

What I know for sure; anything I have experienced in the past is not me, therefore it has no power over me, if I choose to live in the moment of now.

Reflections:

What I Know for Sure
If I change nothing, nothing will ever change

Letting go of what no longer serves me allows me to open the door to that which serves me now.

Reflections:

January 30 — What I Know for Sure

What I Know for Sure
If I change nothing, nothing will ever change

You can move to another state, but you cannot move away from problems. They follow you around until you make peace with them.

Reflections:

What I Know for Sure
If I change nothing, nothing will ever change

Everything in life happens for a reason; sometimes we must explore a little more to find out the reason. Whatever reason you chose to have _____ in your life, what are the lessons that you needed to learn to let go of it, so that it doesn't happen again?

Reflections:

What I Know for Sure

FEBRUARY

What I Know for Sure
If I change nothing, nothing will ever change

When I am confronted with lies about my life, health, or behaviors, I deny these false statements and affirm that my body, my life, and my affairs are operating in accordance with Divine Health and I live in this awareness only.

Reflections:

February 2 — What I Know for Sure

What I Know for Sure
If I change nothing, nothing will ever change

Conscious breathing can create a more peaceful mind and bring about better choices.

Reflections:

What I Know for Sure
If I change nothing, nothing will ever change

Life moves forward whether we are ready or not. So, fasten your seatbelt and prepare for change.

Reflections:

February 4   What I Know for Sure

What I Know for Sure
If I change nothing, nothing will ever change

My behavior was one of skillfully controlling other people. I could be devious, and they did not know it because I presented my mask to the world. Manipulation was my art, until I found out people and places did not want me around anymore and I was extremely lonely. My conduct was unbecoming. I was losing in life. What I know for sure, if I don't change my ways of manipulating others, then nothing will ever change about me, within me, and for me.

Reflections:

What I Know for Sure
If I change nothing, nothing will ever change

It is up to me to choose how I want to be treated by others.

Reflections:

What I Know for Sure
If I change nothing, nothing will ever change

Do not have a dog in your life until you know what your life is, because it's a financial expense. It's a time expense. It creates challenges, if you have no help.

What I know for sure: while having a pet can bring great joy, companionship and unconditional love, it can also create burdens.

Reflections:

What I Know for Sure
If I change nothing, nothing will ever change

Letting go of unfavorable situations, overwhelming experiences, and knowing that life's answers will work out.

Giving it up to the unseen power of God is what I know for sure when I surrender.

Reflections:

February 8   What I Know for Sure

What I Know for Sure
If I change nothing, nothing will ever change

Determining what you want opens the door, and pieces to the puzzle fall into place effortlessly. I no longer need to know exactly how everything will work out ahead of time when I pay attention and trust in the plan God has for me. All will work out in the working out of God's perfect will and knowledge.

Reflections:

What I Know for Sure
If I change nothing, nothing will ever change

What I know for sure: when my trust grows deeper, my intuition blossoms.

Reflections:

February 10 What I Know for Sure

What I Know for Sure
If I change nothing, nothing will ever change

When I feel dis-ease in my body, it is a signal to look deeper for the cause, rather than the cure.

Reflections:

What I Know for Sure
If I change nothing, nothing will ever change

I used to look to others to make my decisions. I even consulted psychics, tarot cards, angel cards, astrologers, and even my hair dresser to make my decisions. It left me crippled and immature. As an adult, I struggled to make life affirming decisions. When I stopped allowing others to make my decisions, I became confident and empowered. It is time to stop letting others determine my path. My best decisions are the ones that I make, even if they don't make sense to anyone else. That is how I know they are mine!

Reflections:

What I Know for Sure
If I change nothing, nothing will ever change

There is a solution to every situation when I remain open to receive the answer.

Staying the course, choosing to push past the pain, I recognize that I must feel, before I can move into a higher place of consciousness. So many people live in the feelings of happy or sad. The need is to tap into deeper levels of feelings. To feel I must give myself permission and trust that it is not going to kill me. The benefits are great and open you to a new level of awareness.

Reflections:

What I Know for Sure
If I change nothing, nothing will ever change

If I never ask, I will never receive.

Sometimes what I need, stands before me like an open door. I just need to knock.

Reflections:

February 14   What I Know for Sure

What I Know for Sure
If I change nothing, nothing will ever change

What some women do not realize, is that they have a fear of releasing through tears.

If I resist opening the flood gates, because of fear, how will I ever stop the flood? Women know on a cellular level, if they allow themselves the opportunity to cry, they are setting themselves free to feel more deeply.

Reflections:

What I Know for Sure
If I change nothing, nothing will ever change

There is a great fear of being out of control.

When I am out of control and releasing through tears, this is when I am most open to knowing my fears, feelings, emotions, and strengths.

Reflections:

February 16   What I Know for Sure

What I Know for Sure
If I change nothing, nothing will ever change

Repeating the same routines daily in an unconscious state of mind, I become lethargic. I choose to get off the merry-go-round and explore with curiosity new ways to expand my life.

Reflections:

What I Know for Sure
If I change nothing, nothing will ever change

Learning to surrender brings true Power.

I feel a sense of letting go, and peace enfolds me.

Reflections:

February 18   What I Know for Sure

What I Know for Sure
If I change nothing, nothing will ever change

During times of turmoil, peace comes. During times of feeling less than, I know for sure I am more than my feelings. I am evolving and expanding and growing.

Reflections:

What I Know for Sure
If I change nothing, nothing will ever change

I am in a glowing field of beauty, love, and light, radiating and vibrating to a higher awareness. I am in tune with Spirit and out of step with the world.

Reflections:

What I Know for Sure
If I change nothing, nothing will ever change

The most valuable gift I can give is being silently present with myself as I become more fully engaged and aware, thus facilitating a deeper awareness and insight within.

Reflections:

What I Know for Sure
If I change nothing, nothing will ever change

Most people think of being alone as a negative aspect, instead of recognizing being alone as a gift. When I honor my time alone, it becomes quality time.

Reflections: How do you spend your alone time?

February 22 — What I Know for Sure

What I Know for Sure
If I change nothing, nothing will ever change

I am worthy, despite all which has transpired in my life. My experiences do not define who I am, unless I allow it. I am worthy of a life filled with love and respect.

Reflections:

What I Know for Sure
If I change nothing, nothing will ever change

When I take time for myself, I connect passionately to my world, and I am inspired. It is as if God is knocking at the door of my consciousness, leading me in the right and perfect way.

Reflections:

February 24   What I Know for Sure

What I Know for Sure
If I change nothing, nothing will ever change

When I feel like I'm being tossed back and forth like a ship in the ocean, that is when I must remember my anchor. I hold onto something solid and firm, so I don't get pulled out to sea. I need not question it. I do not doubt it. My anchor is God. With God in the boat, I smile at the storm.

Reflections:

What I Know for Sure
If I change nothing, nothing will ever change

By living in false beliefs that my life must be filled with challenges to receive good, daily I continue to suffer.

When I am slow to learn life's repeated lessons, the emotional pain is overwhelming, and much greater to bear than the first time around.

The truth is, life is not meant to be hard. It is time for me to choose the path of least resistance.

Reflections:

What I Know for Sure
If I change nothing, nothing will ever change

I am here to express, release, and unfold endless possibilities of the Divine operating in my life. I am here to live life fully expressed.

Reflections:

What I Know for Sure
If I change nothing, nothing will ever change

No longer do I say, "I want, I want, I want." When I am no longer in resistance to receive that which is for me and my highest best, it will come to me.

Reflections:

February 28 — What I Know for Sure

What I Know for Sure
If I change nothing, nothing will ever change

There is power within me, and I am no longer a victim of capricious thinking. I think what I want to think. I think from a spiritual consciousness of power within me. This I know for sure.

Reflections:

What I Know for Sure

MARCH

What I Know for Sure
If I change nothing, nothing will ever change

The Presence is present meaning here and now. There is no absence in the Presence.

I cannot get God to come into my life, because God has never left my life.

Reflections:

March 2 — What I Know for Sure

What I Know for Sure
If I change nothing, nothing will ever change

No house or person can be divided against itself and survive. I know for sure love and service can and will work in bringing this world of homes and people together in Unity.

Reflections:

What I Know for Sure
If I change nothing, nothing will ever change

Finite man engages in war trying to find peace. Infinite man knows that fear must be removed, and that God must enter into a peaceful home.

Reflections:

March 4   What I Know for Sure

What I Know for Sure
If I change nothing, nothing will ever change

I was created in the ecstasy and the inspiration of God. My rhythms reflect God's thinking. I know this for sure!

Reflections:

What I Know for Sure
If I change nothing, nothing will ever change

There is a real live genius within every person struggling for release. Genius is born into every person at birth. Genius is self-bestowed, failure is self-inflicted. What I do with my Divine Inheritance is dependent upon my intensity of my desire to express myself.

Reflections:

March 6 — What I Know for Sure

What I Know for Sure
If I change nothing, nothing will ever change

Death is always balanced with life. As one decreases, the other increases. What is invisible becomes visible and invisible again and again.

Reflections:

What I Know for Sure
If I change nothing, nothing will ever change

Every thought you think is stamped upon your expression, your body, and your face. This is what I know for sure. Happiness attracts happiness, gloom attracts gloom.

Reflections:

March 8 What I Know for Sure

What I Know for Sure
If I change nothing, nothing will ever change

Some people climb a little way up the ladder and then are satisfied; they reach a point at which things are easy and familiar. Ceasing to be curious, they cease to grow. I stretch my mind to wonder, to dream, and to think about what lies beyond the stars. God is an allness and man is an eachness, ever seeking to understand the allness.

Reflections:

What I Know for Sure
If I change nothing, nothing will ever change

It is best to look beyond appearances, to look beyond the prosaic, and to judge righteously.

Reflections:

What I Know for Sure
If I change nothing, nothing will ever change

The more we know, the more we come to see that God is all there is, and that there is an infinite depth of possibility beyond our knowing. My empowerment comes from God.

Reflections:

What I Know for Sure
If I change nothing, nothing will ever change

If we are an idea in the Infinite Mind of God, then we must express ourselves like the symphony in the Mind of the Composer.

Reflections:

What I Know for Sure
If I change nothing, nothing will ever change

The challenges and circumstances of life are shaped and molded almost as musical sounds follow the notes in consciousness. When the sound of negativism is sounded, things begin to shape and move themselves in a negative manner: as within, so without.

Reflections:

What I Know for Sure
If I change nothing, nothing will ever change

I can trace the cause of any illness, injustice or lack. I find that along the lines of causes, there are a few notes off pitch. When I correct the inharmony, I find the symphony coming forth to make all things right. And this is the Divine plan for my life.

Reflections:

What I Know for Sure
If I change nothing, nothing will ever change

The symphony is me, the symphony is you. We are God's melody of life. God, the Infinite composer and director, is singing his song through us. And our part is to cultivate receptivity. I am open and receptive to receiving my good. Are you?

Reflections: Are you open and receptive to receive your good?

What I Know for Sure
If I change nothing, nothing will ever change

I must listen to the progression of harmony and know that despite the challenges and discords of life around me, through spiritual law. I am always what I am created to be.

Reflections:

What I Know for Sure
If I change nothing, nothing will ever change

When I am faced with decisions where there is conflict involving wants versus needs, I must choose wisely. I must enter the stillness, quiet the disturbance in my mind, and listen to my inner compass that holds wisdom. When I go against what I know, it is not wrong, or right. Each choice brings an experience. When I follow my inner compass, my life flows easily, effortlessly, and with less turbulence.

Reflections:

What I Know for Sure
If I change nothing, nothing will ever change

I believe that the spirit in man is mightier than circumstances, that it can and will transcend, even death itself.

Reflections:

What I Know for Sure
If I change nothing, nothing will ever change

We are constantly bombarded with distractions and the fast pace of life. These distractions isolate us from one another. We must seek to be kind, graceful, and responsive. When we act from this consciousness, we create an environment of love filled with inspiration, and know we impact others.

Reflections:

What I Know for Sure
If I change nothing, nothing will ever change

Spending time with those I love is gratifying. I also know that a smile can uplift someone or brighten their day. A hug or a pat on the back is supporting. When I am being myself, I can make a difference in a person's life and influence their life in an entirely new way.

Reflections:

What I Know for Sure
If I change nothing, nothing will ever change

I must strive to maintain a positive attitude of gratitude. I realize that my voice literally has the power to heal or to hurt. The question is: Am I hurting others or am I healing others? Every person who enters my circle, I choose to love them, and they will exit my presence feeling at peace with themselves, the world and everyone in it. I can make a difference in a person's life when they enter my space.

Reflections:

What I Know for Sure
If I change nothing, nothing will ever change

I believe that when we came here to the earth plane, we had all the tools we need. We must reclaim our gifts in order to use them. We must realize who we are.

What I know for sure; I have the strength and courage within to achieve greatness. My purpose is to reclaim it and use it for good.

Reflections:

What I Know for Sure
If I change nothing, nothing will ever change

We have stories that run through our minds continuously. It is time to recognize we are not those stories. They are stories placed in our minds as lies, told to us by other people.

What I know for sure; any negative thoughts in my head are simply false beliefs. The truth is, I am a perfect child of God.

Reflections:

What I Know for Sure
If I change nothing, nothing will ever change

Believing false untruths about myself or my situation or allowing these negatives to overtake my confidence, will find me in the darkness with despair and it will be difficult to get out.

What I know for sure; sometimes I find myself in darkness and I must consciously choose to come back to the light through prayer, meditation, and silence. The choice is mine.

Reflections:

March 24 — What I Know for Sure

What I Know for Sure
If I change nothing, nothing will ever change

Time is the only thing we cannot get more of therefore, spend it wisely.

Reflections:

What I Know for Sure
If I change nothing, nothing will ever change

Why do I continue to engage in negative behaviors thinking that I am getting away with it and no one sees? Someone is always watching in the higher realms of spiritual consciousness. There are watchers everywhere. There are gatekeepers who keep the order of the universe even when we think we are getting away with ugly deeds.

What I know for sure, is nothing goes unnoticed.

Reflections:

March 26 — What I Know for Sure

What I Know for Sure
If I change nothing, nothing will ever change

Often, we search for a person or place to complete us and make us feel safe and at home, when the real safety and comfort comes from within.

What I know for sure; my home is not with another person or a specific place, it is always with me…in my heart.

Reflections:

What I Know for Sure
If I change nothing, nothing will ever change

I affirm, I am awesome, and I deny anyone who says otherwise!

Reflections:

What I Know for Sure
If I change nothing, nothing will ever change

When we love the things about ourselves and accept the things we don't like, it opens our eyes and gives us as awareness to change, grow, and improve.

What I know for sure; self-love means embracing and accepting everything about me, including the things I may not like.

I am perfect in God's eyes.

Reflections:

What I Know for Sure
If I change nothing, nothing will ever change

I have been my own worst critic. It is time to recognize and acknowledge my assets, talents, and abilities. I accept and acknowledge my gifts and contributions to the world.

Reflections:

What I Know for Sure
If I change nothing, nothing will ever change

On the path of life, I often feel lost or unsure of my purpose. My purpose is really me and not everyone else around me.

What I know for sure; I am one with the loving light of God, and my sole purpose is to find my way home.

Reflections:

What I Know for Sure
If I change nothing, nothing will ever change

Everyone suffers with a 'not being good enough' mentality, which is lies we have chosen to believe.

What I know for sure, I am worthy and deserving of good in my life. I must believe it and receive it.

Reflections:

What I Know for Sure

APRIL

What I Know for Sure
If I change nothing, nothing will ever change

It is easy for most people to give. It makes them feel good about themselves, and yet they often reject receiving when the favor of giving is returned.

What I know for sure; learning to receive is as important as giving. By learning to receive, I have more to give as my heart is full.

Reflections:

What I Know for Sure
If I change nothing, nothing will ever change

We often look to the outside world for the answers. Pausing and taking time to go within is our unique way of receiving guidance for our path to become clear.

What I know for sure, all the wisdom I need is within me, I just need to ask, listen, and patiently wait.

Reflections:

What I Know for Sure
If I change nothing, nothing will ever change

When I take responsibility for my life through connection with Spirit, life flows with ease and grace. When I'm not in alignment and choose to blame others, the road is treacherous.

What I know for sure; life happens through me, not to me.

Reflections:

April 4 — What I Know for Sure

What I Know for Sure
If I change nothing, nothing will ever change

Life is simple, we choose to complicate it.

Reflections:

What I Know for Sure
If I change nothing, nothing will ever change

No matter what happens in the world, no matter what happens to me, or what pressing issue is before me, the only thing that really counts is what happens within my own mind. When my thoughts are positive, and my mind is at peace, nothing can disturb me.

Reflections:

What I Know for Sure
If I change nothing, nothing will ever change

When I am centered within myself and centered within the Divine flow, I walk easily through experiences in the world by faith and not by fear. When I am centered within myself, I am in charge, and I no longer worry over the past, the future or the economy, not the clock or the calendar, not worldly possessions or the need to conform. This is a marvelous realization that works wonders for myself, because this is what I know for sure.

Reflections:

What I Know for Sure
If I change nothing, nothing will ever change

I hold the power to make or break, to succeed or fail, to enjoy good health or to be sick, lonely, and afraid, to release the beauty or to block the eternal infinite energy from which all good things come forth. This is what I know for sure.

Reflections:

What I Know for Sure
If I change nothing, nothing will ever change

God's Will: God's Will is the ceaseless longing of the Creator to perfect himself in all his creation, and this longing can be channeled into an irresistible force for health, for wise guidance, and for sufficient and continuous supply.

Reflections:

What I Know for Sure
If I change nothing, nothing will ever change

The Divine urge within every human is to fulfill. It is the evidence of the Will of God in me and for me. What I know for sure like faith, God's Will is a phase of the Divine Process within all persons; it is the stirring of the God-self within. I must treat the Will like I treat faith, like an activity of Divine Mind.

Reflections:

What I Know for Sure
If I change nothing, nothing will ever change

What people don't like about me is often what they don't like about themselves. What other people think about me is none of my business. I am focused on living my life.

Reflections:

What I Know for Sure
If I change nothing, nothing will ever change

People or situations appear to assist me during my life. When my course is in harmony, I recognize I am on the correct path.

Reflections:

April 12   What I Know for Sure

What I Know for Sure
If I change nothing, nothing will ever change

I can't change what happened yesterday and I certainly can't change what happened last year. Every day is a new day. Regardless of what happened yesterday or last year, I choose how I feel now!

Reflections:

What I Know for Sure
If I change nothing, nothing will ever change

Our bodies are self-healing machines. When we stay in the flow with positive thoughts, trust in the healing process of the body, and maintain the belief that we are a perfect child of God, healing can and will occur.

We must dare to ask the question, "What was happening in my life or thoughts before the dis-ease manifested in my body?

Reflections:

What I Know for Sure
If I change nothing, nothing will ever change

My body is a perfect gift from God and it is my responsibility to maintain its health through nourishing, nurturing, and applying generous doses of loving self-care.

Reflections:

What I Know for Sure
If I change nothing, nothing will ever change

Life is a game, don't take yourself too seriously, play the game wisely, and reap life's rewards joyously.

Reflections:

April 16   What I Know for Sure

What I Know for Sure
If I change nothing, nothing will ever change

How things work out is a mystery when I look at circumstances through my little lens. However, when I see through spiritual glasses, I have faith and trust in the unseen, and miracles do occur. What miracles have you seen?

Reflections:

What I Know for Sure
If I change nothing, nothing will ever change

Nothing ever stays the same except God and God's love. Embrace and expect change. Change is good!

Reflections:

What I Know for Sure
If I change nothing, nothing will ever change

The Will of God: I may be temporarily out of money, I may be temporarily out of a job, I may experience physical and mental problems, or I may be lost. But, what I know for sure is that I can never be out of the Mind of God.

I can never be out of the Infinite process of Divine Mind. I am the creative expression of God and God's Will, and I am sustained by this Will.

Reflections:

What I Know for Sure
If I change nothing, nothing will ever change

Remembering that if you don't trust yourself, how can you expect to trust someone else? Trusting others is easier when we first learn to trust in ourselves.

Reflections:

What I Know for Sure
If I change nothing, nothing will ever change

If God loves me unconditionally, who am I not to love myself?

Reflections:

What I Know for Sure
If I change nothing, nothing will ever change

Addictions are behaviors that are excessive in nature. They prohibit me from performing what I am meant to be doing. What are your addictive behaviors?

Reflections:

What I Know for Sure
If I change nothing, nothing will ever change

For me to rebuild trust and heal wounds, I must remain open and transparent whenever possible. Are you transparent?

Reflections:

What I Know for Sure
If I change nothing, nothing will ever change

Procrastination is a five-syllable word for sloth. The only thing keeping me stuck is me. What is keeping you stuck?

Reflections:

What I Know for Sure
If I change nothing, nothing will ever change

On Silence: In the silence, I listen and read only what is written in my heart. Without the distractions of many things around vying for my attention, especially my thoughts, it is the distractions of speech, whether I write it or speak it. There is a place in the silence which is the gap. That sacred space is so precious, just as I am. I am extremely precious, beautiful, and vulnerable. This sacred space calls for a slow, conscious response to life, rather than the hurried anxious patterns that I am accustomed to. What I know for sure: I allow myself the gift of silence in my heart space.

Reflections:

What I Know for Sure
If I change nothing, nothing will ever change

Spending time in nature recharges my batteries, brings me back to the innermost center of alignment with Spirit. What I know for sure; how vitally important it is to reconnect with the forces of nature.

Reflections:

What I Know for Sure
If I change nothing, nothing will ever change

When I remain in alignment with right thoughts, words, and actions, my light brilliantly shines, and darkness cannot enter.

I must nourish myself with God's love daily.

Reflections:

What I Know for Sure
If I change nothing, nothing will ever change

During my darkest times when I am filled with deep despair, the best solutions emerge when I surrender to God, knowing better times await me.

What I know for sure; the greatest challenges result in the biggest rewards. I embrace new ideas for change.

Reflections:

What I Know for Sure
If I change nothing, nothing will ever change

My internal strength, faith, and belief in God's love are pivotal key assets. These gifts always light my way.

Reflections:

What I Know for Sure
If I change nothing, nothing will ever change

Other people's beliefs, including family and society-at-large, have led me down the wrong path. What I know for sure; my beliefs arise out of my own experiences.

I release limiting beliefs and replace them with positive experiences of Truth that God meant for me to experience. The beliefs which best serve me arise from my own experience.

Reflections:

What I Know for Sure
If I change nothing, nothing will ever change

When in doubt, feel it out. Get out of your head and get into your heart. Close the door on the chatter in your mind, then feel into your heart-body. When you do not feel a full body YES, know it is a capital NO!

Your body holds wisdom. Listen to it.

Reflections:

What I Know for Sure

MAY

What I Know for Sure
If I change nothing, nothing will ever change

Our journeys never end, so let go of arriving at the destination and enjoy the adventure.

Reflections:

May 2 — What I Know for Sure

What I Know for Sure
If I change nothing, nothing will ever change

Tears do not always represent weakness. Tears sometimes convey present feelings of my own truth. I can be vulnerable and strong at the same time. I can stand in my power, during my vulnerability.

Reflections:

What I Know for Sure
If I change nothing, nothing will ever change

Tears allow me the freedom to express my power. Tears allow me the opportunity to cleanse, to heal, to dissolve barriers of negativity into positive streams of my light.

I embrace my tears.

Reflections:

What I Know for Sure
If I change nothing, nothing will ever change

Please do not try to hug me or force me to stop crying; can't you see, I'm in my power.

Tears create for me a dynamic force of awakening to my inner power.

Reflections:

What I Know for Sure
If I change nothing, nothing will ever change

Micro managing my children's lives and protecting them from consequences delays their growth. Children must be allowed freedom of thought and choice, which opens their creativity for navigating life. It teaches them to be responsible and self-confident.

Reflections:

What I Know for Sure
If I change nothing, nothing will ever change

Through the years, I have been fed false beliefs and given ideas of others that do not agree with my eternal nature of Oneness.

It takes courage to recognize, realize and reclaim myself with this truth; I am a child of God!

Reflections:

What I Know for Sure
If I change nothing, nothing will ever change

Decorating or remodeling a room in my home teaches me how to apply my talents and gifts, to re-direct my thinking, and to reconstruct my life in vibrant ways that are healthy and harmonious.

I co-create with God, designing my life in an abundant way.

Reflections:

What I Know for Sure
If I change nothing, nothing will ever change

I utilize my successful experiences of designing and creating good in my life to propel my mind forward.

I must choose favorable instruments from my tool box to support and create the life I choose to live.

Reflections:

What I Know for Sure
If I change nothing, nothing will ever change

There is that part of myself which remains unknown and sequestered. Sometimes it influences parts of my life.

It is hidden from you and the world.

What I know for sure is that I am no longer willing to create and cause suffering in my life. I now embrace all of myself with respect and allow my light to shine, especially over the dark parts.

Reflections:

What I Know for Sure
If I change nothing, nothing will ever change

Sometimes my mind runs around with undisciplined emotions, often creating havoc and making me suffer. When I remember to shine my bright light into the world, unruly emotions no longer have power over me and I know for sure that when I always commit to finding the Divine level within myself.

I become fully empowered to create a life of purpose, joy, and meaning.

Reflections:

What I Know for Sure
If I change nothing, nothing will ever change

I am committed to empowering myself to create a life of purpose, joy, and meaning.

Reflections:

What I Know for Sure
If I change nothing, nothing will ever change

As a mother the greatest gift I can give my children is recognizing and seeing them as they truly are, as spiritual beings and holding them in the perfection of God.

Reflections:

What I Know for Sure
If I change nothing, nothing will ever change

When I take time to examine my emotions, attitudes, and general well-being, then I know for sure that my healing has begun.

Reflections:

What I Know for Sure
If I change nothing, nothing will ever change

I must continuously pursue the study and development of my inner self, seeking to know myself, thus to know God in an intimate way.

Reflections:

What I Know for Sure
If I change nothing, nothing will ever change

I am born knowing this Truth; that my awareness is deep within and I understand the nature of such potent energetic power that I carry.

Reflections:

What I Know for Sure
If I change nothing, nothing will ever change

Because I am constantly awakening the Divinity within, developing and unfolding my inner psychic and intuitive abilities, I know that falling back asleep into old patterns of negative behaviors is not an option! Today I make choices that further expands my growth.

Reflections:

What I Know for Sure
If I change nothing, nothing will ever change

I can hang on to my children as a life preserver, hiding behind them, neglecting self. However, at some point, it's time to risk letting go in order to find my own purpose.

Reflections:

What I Know for Sure
If I change nothing, nothing will ever change

Often, as parents we want to live our lives vicariously through our children, instead of moving into our own strengths and possibilities long neglected and forgotten.

I choose to honor myself, realizing and recognizing my desires.

Reflections: Now list 10 things I would do for myself to feed my soul.

What I Know for Sure
If I change nothing, nothing will ever change

Parents on the side lines at their child's events, often try to be in their body, or wish they were a child again, so they might achieve through their children, what they did not themselves achieve.

What I know for sure; if you want to play a sport, or further your education, join an adult league, take a course, and lead by example. My child's life is not my life to live; it's theirs!

Reflections:

What I Know for Sure
If I change nothing, nothing will ever change

Caring about what others think, say, or do, often leads me to feel disappointed in myself. What I know for sure is I can reclaim my life by stepping into my power, even if it doesn't' look the way others see it.

People are afraid to move away from society's views and expectations of family life, the "status quo" or norm.

Reflections:

What I Know for Sure
If I change nothing, nothing will ever change

I must not feel afraid or disappointed for stepping into my own power. What I feel is a sense of worthiness and the ability to reclaim my life, even if it doesn't look the way it is supposed to look. I must know for sure that it looks good to me, and that I am doing this for self and not for others.

Reflections:

May 22 — What I Know for Sure

What I Know for Sure
If I change nothing, nothing will ever change

Do not feel disappointed or afraid to step into your own power and to reclaim your life, even if it doesn't look the way others expect it to, you must know for sure that you are not afraid, and it looks good to you. You're doing this for self.

Reflections:

What I Know for Sure
If I change nothing, nothing will ever change

People just do, do, do, living a busy life without being present in it. What I know for sure is we are human beings, not human doers.

Reflections: How can I be more present today?

What I Know for Sure
If I change nothing, nothing will ever change

If I am searching for a different job, different weather, a different environment, and real friends, I am seeking to escape.

When I am unhappy, feeling lonely and experiencing low self-esteem, no self-love, and a sense of unworthiness, I may look to the external world to fill my interior world. I know true happiness and love comes from developing a relationship with Spirit. The best living comes from the inside out.

Reflections:

What I Know for Sure
If I change nothing, nothing will ever change

People who diminish my value and find fault with me to make themselves feel better are not the people I want in my life.

Reflections:

What I Know for Sure
If I change nothing, nothing will ever change

When challenges or changes occur, I must learn how to trust my own intuition and inner guidance. Then I am able to make clear decisions and follow through.

Reflections:

What I Know for Sure
If I change nothing, nothing will ever change

I speak with the authority of One who knows and the Power of Spirit Divine. I know for sure that unlimited good is unfolding in my life and I accept this good for me and everyone. I take dominion over my thoughts and feelings and speak with Divine authority.

Reflections:

What I Know for Sure
If I change nothing, nothing will ever change

I take care of others and often forget about taking care of myself. I must remember that I am the most important person in my life to me today. I come first and foremost. I matter in my life.

Reflections:

What I Know for Sure
If I change nothing, nothing will ever change

I must do the inner work.

Reflections:

What I Know for Sure
If I change nothing, nothing will ever change

For years, abuse, batter, and neglect were my constant companions. I clung to the pain doled out by my partners, friends, and those who were abused, neglected, and broken. I am now learning to recognize the pattern of abuse in my life based on my past. My truth is the decision that I make for today. I am learning to love myself and recognize that I am the most important person in my life.

Reflections:

What I Know for Sure
If I change nothing, nothing will ever change

Every thought, feeling, or action I engage in …is involved in the unfolding events on earth. I choose to participate and make a difference in my world. I choose to think from a high-level thinking; I choose transcendental thinking.

Reflections:

What I Know for Sure

JUNE

What I Know for Sure
If I change nothing, nothing will ever change

My thoughts and choices make a difference, and when I choose to think from the highest thought possible, I shift the direction of my entire life.

Reflections:

June 2 What I Know for Sure

What I Know for Sure
If I change nothing, nothing will ever change

I was born to give forgiveness and to share grace.

Reflections:

What I Know for Sure
If I change nothing, nothing will ever change

My word is my bond. If I break my word, I shatter a commitment and demolish a union forever. I know for sure the power of right speech, and I express love with my words.

Reflections:

What I Know for Sure
If I change nothing, nothing will ever change

We are all one, there are no separations. There is always an answer to every challenge, every difficulty, and every conflict. When we push beyond this separation between us and the answer to our need, Oneness will unfold.

Reflections:

What I Know for Sure
If I change nothing, nothing will ever change

When I step across the illusive line of separation, I enter into a land of milk and honey and manifest all that which is for me by Divine Inheritance.

Reflections:

What I Know for Sure
If I change nothing, nothing will ever change

Lack, limitations and self-limiting beliefs keep me in a state of inner conflict. I need to break through the shell of my limited self and claim my unlimited self. I speak the words of truth for myself. I say, "My good will unfold, my perfect health will manifest."

Reflections:

What I Know for Sure
If I change nothing, nothing will ever change

I have within me the power and potential to rise above every situation and deal with any challenge. This is the fundamental Divine law of the Divinity of who I am.

Reflections:

What I Know for Sure
If I change nothing, nothing will ever change

If I'm not thinking good thoughts about the world and about people, I'm probably thinking negatively about myself, and I cannot afford that. I cannot afford to hold negative thoughts about myself. If I do, it's because I am blocking my own Divine flow. The need is to let go, and let flow.

Reflections:

What I Know for Sure
If I change nothing, nothing will ever change

When I give thanks, it will raise my consciousness to a level to where I can experience the activity of, and the support of the dynamic presence of God within me.

Reflections:

What I Know for Sure
If I change nothing, nothing will ever change

I am a unique individualization of God; to realize this truth about myself is to lift my attitude and relate to myself on an entirely different, transcendental level.

Reflections:

What I Know for Sure
If I change nothing, nothing will ever change

I believe that all people are important, and I deal with each person realizing that they are important. They are important to God. They are important to life. I give thanks for the gift of sight to see the good in others.

Reflections:

What I Know for Sure
If I change nothing, nothing will ever change

If I engage in sexual behavior immediately after meeting someone, I've lost myself in a vulnerable way without ever understanding myself or my partner. Regrettably, I am unable to recover my sense of self-worth and dignity.

Reflections:

What I Know for Sure
If I change nothing, nothing will ever change

If I enter an intimate relationship too soon, I could be giving away a sacred piece of myself out of fear, loneliness, and pressure from which I may not recover. It is best to be patient and allow the relationship to unfold in a comfortable way. If I am loved and respected, they will wait.

Reflections:

What I Know for Sure
If I change nothing, nothing will ever change

If my expectations are for another to raise my self-esteem or to complete me, I am only fooling myself. I know I am complete as a child of God. I expect to be with someone whose consciousness is equal to or greater than mine.

Reflections:

What I Know for Sure
If I change nothing, nothing will ever change

My expectations are never too high. If I maintain the belief of my Truth, I am deserving of all that is good.

Reflections:

What I Know for Sure
If I change nothing, nothing will ever change

I have the capacity to love all; however, physical intimacy is reserved, sacred, and to be entered into with wisdom, trust, and faith.

Reflections:

What I Know for Sure
If I change nothing, nothing will ever change

To love another, I must accept them as they are, unconditionally, and not try to change then.

Reflections:

What I Know for Sure
If I change nothing, nothing will ever change

I must completely love myself, including the shadow self that I don't like. A difference between liking and loving is if you don't like yourself, you're not going to be able to love all parts of yourself. Liking is a feeling, love is a willingness to let love flow through you. As I recognize and accept those differing parts, I have the choice to change certain aspects of myself.

Awareness is the first step to change.

Reflections:

What I Know for Sure
If I change nothing, nothing will ever change

If I perceive myself as unlovable and unworthy, of a loving relationship, then I am attracting the same from another.

What I know for sure is that like attracts like.

Reflections:

What I Know for Sure
If I change nothing, nothing will ever change

If I am not committed to myself, I cannot expect anyone else to be.

Reflections:

What I Know for Sure
If I change nothing, nothing will ever change

Fear of success can be more debilitating than fear of failure.

I must own my success and be proud of it.

This means acknowledging my brilliance instead of denying it.

Reflections:

What I Know for Sure
If I change nothing, nothing will ever change

To attract individuals that I desire or a partner to come into my life, I must become the person I want to be with.

Reflections:

What I Know for Sure
If I change nothing, nothing will ever change

Using people or experiences as an excuse for dissatisfaction in my life, instead of being honest, slows down my forward progress. I am responsible for my own growth!

Reflections:

What I Know for Sure
If I change nothing, nothing will ever change

If I encounter a negative reaction to someone for no apparent reason, I am most served by pausing and asking, "What is it in her which is something about myself I do not like?"

Remembering people are simply mirrors, reflecting information needed to assist my own growth and the expansion of self, I use the mirrors to remind me of my positive qualities also.

Reflections:

What I Know for Sure
If I change nothing, nothing will ever change

Approaching each day with "I wonder what surprises will delight me today" creates an eagerness and awareness of what is happening around me.

Reflections:

What I Know for Sure
If I change nothing, nothing will ever change

What is my quest? Who is the seeker in me which continues as is today? What am I constantly striving for?

I know for sure; that I become conscious of my new nature, current nature and old nature. I constantly seek change and growth.

Reflections:

What I Know for Sure
If I change nothing, nothing will ever change

My first commitment is to self and to God, as I must love myself to be able to create miracles with a partner.

Reflections:

What I Know for Sure
If I change nothing, nothing will ever change

Sex is a physical exchange of energy for pleasure or procreation. A loving union is a conscious energetic connection shared in a sacred way between two individuals committed to their partners' greatest good and spiritual growth.

Reflections:

What I Know for Sure
If I change nothing, nothing will ever change

A person may go from one relationship to another, seeking in sex that which can only be found in love. Sex without love can lead only to loneliness, insecurity, and downright stifling possessiveness.

Reflections:

What I Know for Sure
If I change nothing, nothing will ever change

Pain is not natural. Pain is life's way of getting our attention. When we have achieved a higher level of awareness, it is the first step toward healing. When pain comes to interrupt and erupt like a volcano in our life, we must stop doing whatever is causing it, and begin to activate our choices by doing whatever it takes to transform pain. What I know for sure is pain is not natural.

Reflections:

What I Know for Sure

JULY

What I Know for Sure
If I change nothing, nothing will ever change

Pain comes as a way of interrupting the negative patterns in our lives. Pain is not natural. It indicates a time to refrain.

Reflections:

July 2 — What I Know for Sure

What I Know for Sure
If I change nothing, nothing will ever change

Sometimes I am not always right, and sometimes I am not always wrong. It could be time to be humble. I go within and know it is time for breathing in Truth with the sacred breath.

Reflections:

What I Know for Sure
If I change nothing, nothing will ever change

I know that living with a clear conscience raises our consciousness to resonate with higher vibrations.

I live life with intention.

Reflections:

What I Know for Sure
If I change nothing, nothing will ever change

Many are waking up to the Truth of who they are and see how separate they have treated life. What I know for sure; it is time to get out of the shadow and dance the song of life.

Reflections:

What I Know for Sure
If I change nothing, nothing will ever change

I trust that where I am is where I am supposed to be. And where I am supposed to be at this moment is perfect in all its seeming imperfections. I live in the Now.

Reflections:

What I Know for Sure
If I change nothing, nothing will ever change

When I am confronted with a challenge, through faith it makes sense to walk through the challenge instead of walking away and trying to avoid it. When I walk steadfastly, I make the challenge my gift. I become one with my surroundings in a more harmonious and balanced way.

Reflections:

What I Know for Sure
If I change nothing, nothing will ever change

When I am caught up in my own world, it is because I think that everything is separate from me. I am One with the Infinite flow, and life moves through me now.

Reflections:

What I Know for Sure
If I change nothing, nothing will ever change

I follow the the road of my heart. The road of the heart is the Divine road that connects me with Good Orderly Direction.

Reflections:

What I Know for Sure
If I change nothing, nothing will ever change

We all have flaws. When I see the flaws in someone else, I am seeing that flaw in myself. We are all one, and the spot in my friend's eye, is also in my own eye.

Reflections:

July 10   What I Know for Sure

What I Know for Sure
If I change nothing, nothing will ever change

When I approach an uncomfortable conversation with love, the results can produce great rewards.

Reflections:

What I Know for Sure
If I change nothing, nothing will ever change

I must get honest with myself and answer the tough questions. Time to get real, I am worth it!

Reflections:

What I Know for Sure
If I change nothing, nothing will ever change

Anything I have experienced in my past is not me. My past does not define me, and my past has no power over me, unless I allow it. I step out of old ways of thinking, being, and believing to create my new reality.

Reflections:

What I Know for Sure
If I change nothing, nothing will ever change

By denying old limiting beliefs which have held me hostage, I erase and dissolve the power they have over me. Then I affirm the truth of who I am; a whole, healthy, and perfect child of God.

Reflections:

July 14 — What I Know for Sure

What I Know for Sure
If I change nothing, nothing will ever change

Today I recognize my strength, courage and power. By owning all parts of myself, I am able to propel myself forward on my journey with confidence knowing I am always supported by Divine Guidance.

Reflections:

What I Know for Sure
If I change nothing, nothing will ever change

I feel there is a fine line sharing wisdom with my adult children as I want them to live life on their own terms.

However, with honest communication and coming from a place of love, I gift them with thoughtful questions to ponder instead of imposing my beliefs on them.

What I know for sure is that we all possess wisdom to ask the right questions and to listen. However no one likes to be told what to do.

Reflections:

What I Know for Sure
If I change nothing, nothing will ever change

While my children will always be my babies, I recognize they are on their journey and I allow them the freedom to make decisions.

Reflections:

What I Know for Sure
If I change nothing, nothing will ever change

Resistance to follow inner guidance may lead to missing out on unexpected surprises.

Reflections:

What I Know for Sure
If I change nothing, nothing will ever change

I once was told to repeat daily, "God Loves Me" and then to feel it internally and observe my feelings. Saying God Loves me repeatedly changes my negative thoughts to positive thoughts and I feel the changes in my life. What I know for sure is when I hold this belief in my heart, my world responds favorably.

Reflections:

What I Know for Sure
If I change nothing, nothing will ever change

When I live in the awareness of Oneness with God and recognize that I am loved and supported, my confidence shines.

I feel stronger, and people are drawn to this quality in myself.

Reflections:

July 20   What I Know for Sure

What I Know for Sure
If I change nothing, nothing will ever change

My angels and spirit guides are always around me waiting for my request, because without it they cannot help.

Ask and it is given!

Reflections:

What I Know for Sure
If I change nothing, nothing will ever change

One of the easiest and nicest gifts you can give to yourself is to surround yourself with loving and kind people whenever possible.

Reflections:

What I Know for Sure
If I change nothing, nothing will ever change

I am at peace with myself, the world, and everyone in it. I am blessed by God's love. I want to go deeper within myself. I want more God. I am willing, receptive, and open to receiving my good. I trust you Infinite Spirit. I am never alone. I know that you are with me Spirit.

Reflections:

What I Know for Sure
If I change nothing, nothing will ever change

Lying retards my ability to live life in its fullest. I think lying covers my inadequacies and low self-esteem. Until I search out the flaws and expose my character defects and short-comings, how can I expect anyone to be honest with or trust me.

The truth is always revealed in the end.

Reflections:

What I Know for Sure
If I change nothing, nothing will ever change

When you share love with your partner, you can say what you need to say and not feel threatened.

Reflections:

What I Know for Sure
If I change nothing, nothing will ever change

I am poised, peaceful, and harmonious.

No longer do I need to defend myself. I let go of the defensive side of my nature, which goes back to childhood, in my family, and the outside world. I don't need to defend myself, because I am One with all life and all power, with God, the good, the omnipotent.

Reflections:

What I Know for Sure
If I change nothing, nothing will ever change

By stuffing my words and feelings, over time I am unable to live life with freedom to soar. When I speak my truth, negative thoughts and beliefs in my head lose power over me.

Reflections:

What I Know for Sure
If I change nothing, nothing will ever change

By acknowledging who I really am, I am capable of living my best life, the life God intended for me to experience, filled with power, strength, courage, peace, joy, and love.

Reflections:

What I Know for Sure
If I change nothing, nothing will ever change

As I uncover layers of truth about myself, multiple feelings overwhelm me. I become afraid, until I pause, reflect, and recall that this is part of the upward process to love.

Reflections:

What I Know for Sure
If I change nothing, nothing will ever change

When I am willing to give myself permission to _____.
I push beyond old ways of thinking. I choose good in my life now!

Reflections:

What I Know for Sure
If I change nothing, nothing will ever change

When I gaze into my eyes and notice the light beginning to dim, I search within and recognize that my current situation or relationship brings pain. This discomfort within my body is reevaluated, washed out, cleansed, and purified. I re-ignite my flame.

I have dominion over my own reality.

Reflections:

What I Know for Sure
If I change nothing, nothing will ever change

Patience teaches me to pause. Therefore, my words, thoughts and actions unfold in pleasantly surprising ways. By trying to force events to happen now or force others to do things my way, this has led to disappointments which by using some restraint and patience could have been avoided.

Reflections:

What I Know for Sure

AUGUST

What I Know for Sure
If I change nothing, nothing will ever change

If I perceive my life half full, it fills up quickly with more and more good.

Reflections:

August 2 What I Know for Sure

What I Know for Sure
If I change nothing, nothing will ever change

Every day I have breath, I have life, and I continue to make a difference in the world. Live each moment with passion, with purpose.

Reflections:

What I Know for Sure
If I change nothing, nothing will ever change

Today I understand that my courage to step outside of my comfort zone was the beginning of a new way of life. My life is now filled with peace, contentment, and love.

Reflections:

What I Know for Sure
If I change nothing, nothing will ever change

Never quit your daydream. Unrealized dreams create discomfort in every cell, atom and electron of my body over time. I must now believe that anything I desire is possible. Then I can begin to believe without doubt that my dreams will come true. Live each dream backwards, see the outcome first, then trust, and have faith that it can manifest.

Reflections:

What I Know for Sure
If I change nothing, nothing will ever change

When presented with a second chance, I embrace the moment, letting go of old beliefs and previous perceived obstacles. I step into limitless possibilities with an open mind.

Reflections:

August 6 What I Know for Sure

What I Know for Sure
If I change nothing, nothing will ever change

I never give up, as all seeming failures are just one step toward finding the solution.

Reflections:

What I Know for Sure
If I change nothing, nothing will ever change

When I am willing to delve into the shadow aspects of self, I free myself from doubt, fear, and uncertainty.

Reflections:

What I Know for Sure
If I change nothing, nothing will ever change

There are no do overs; I cannot go back to being age 10 when I am age 30. I cannot wish for the past, it's finished. It's time to be an adult.

Reflections:

What I Know for Sure
If I change nothing, nothing will ever change

I leave the past in the past. I do not relive it in my mind, fear of what may or what may not come. I know for sure that negative energy comes from worrying over the past. I stay in the moment. I put my trust in God, until peace is restored. I do not have to fight anyone alone. It is a perception of what is perfect. What I know for sure; only God is perfect, humans are not!

Reflections:

What I Know for Sure
If I change nothing, nothing will ever change

Discomfort and isolation may feel uncomfortable; however, by allowing myself to endure discomfort with discipline, I am able to burst through to new levels.

Reflections:

What I Know for Sure
If I change nothing, nothing will ever change

God's messages for me are unique and personal. Therefore, looking outside of myself, I will not acquire the answers I require. My daily practice of prayer and meditation are the most effective way to receive.

Reflections:

What I Know for Sure
If I change nothing, nothing will ever change

When I align myself with God through right thoughts, right words, and right actions, I move through life with joy, ease and grace. Any obstacles seem to move effortlessly out of my path.

Reflections:

What I Know for Sure
If I change nothing, nothing will ever change

Each dawn is a new beginning. Visualizing the day I wish to create before I rise or during meditation provides clarity which leads to more productivity and essentially more time.

Reflections:

What I Know for Sure
If I change nothing, nothing will ever change

My internal life creates my outward manifestation.

I must watch my thoughts diligently to be sure they are positive and in my highest best, if I wish to have the life I want to live.

Reflections:

What I Know for Sure
If I change nothing, nothing will ever change

The answers I seek are often disguised by recurring signs in the world around me. Approach life like a game; stay alert, awake, and aware to play like a champion.

Reflections:

August 16 — What I Know for Sure

What I Know for Sure
If I change nothing, nothing will ever change

Through love and compassion, I can begin to nurture myself, to plant seeds that gingerly need to be watered. Over a period of time, I will see sprouts take place. Growth is an especially important part of self-discovery.

Reflections:

What I Know for Sure
If I change nothing, nothing will ever change

Shedding the old form of self seems frightening at first, but it is necessary to breaking free of the old mold. Today I am stepping into one of my new creations with endless possibilities.

Reflections:

August 18   What I Know for Sure

What I Know for Sure
If I change nothing, nothing will ever change

I know living with a clear conscience raises my consciousness to resonate with higher vibrations.

I live life with intention.

Reflections:

What I Know for Sure
If I change nothing, nothing will ever change

Many are waking up to the Truth of who they are and seeing how separate they have treated life. What I know for sure; it is time to get out of the shadow and dance the song of life.

Reflections:

What I Know for Sure
If I change nothing, nothing will ever change

I trust that where I am, it is where I am supposed to be, and where I am supposed to be at this moment is perfect in all its seeming imperfections. I live in the Now.

Reflections:

What I Know for Sure
If I change nothing, nothing will ever change

When I am confronted with a challenge, through Faith, it makes sense to walk through the challenge instead of walking away trying to avoid it. When I walk steadfastly through, I make the challenge my gift. I become one with my surroundings in a more harmonious and balanced way.

Reflections:

What I Know for Sure
If I change nothing, nothing will ever change

When I am caught up in my own world, it is because I think that everything is separate from me. I am One with the Infinite Flow and life moves through me now.

Reflections:

What I Know for Sure
If I change nothing, nothing will ever change

I have profound masculine energy that gives me an urge for self-conquest, which have been a lifelong pursuit for my soul. I call for awareness, single mindedness, and willingness. I've undertaken my passage with compassion and total trust. I have courage, I have dedication, but at the same time, I know that I must always align self with the Higher Self.

Reflections:

August 24

What I Know for Sure
If I change nothing, nothing will ever change

I must get honest with myself and answer the tough questions, before I am able to elicit the change in my life I hunger for.

Time to get real, I am worth it!

Reflections:

What I Know for Sure
If I change nothing, nothing will ever change

Anything I have experienced in my past is not me, does not define me and has no power over me unless I allow it.

The time is now to step out of old ways of thinking, being, and believing and to create what I want to be my new reality.

Reflections:

What I Know for Sure
If I change nothing, nothing will ever change

When I am willing to give myself permission to receive good, I push beyond the old erroneous ways of thinking.

I choose good in my life now!

Reflections:

What I Know for Sure
If I change nothing, nothing will ever change

Every event in my life is simply a stepping stone for what lies ahead, therefore, it is my responsibility to obtain the golden nugget from any situation whether it is a challenge or a blessing, so I can climb higher and reach higher levels of awareness.

There is always a diamond in the rough.

Reflections:

What I Know for Sure
If I change nothing, nothing will ever change

I stand in my light exposing my true authentic self and others benefit without even knowing. My light must remain bright to create change in the world.

Reflections:

What I Know for Sure
If I change nothing, nothing will ever change

My internal life creates my outward manifestation.

I must watch my thoughts diligently to be sure they are positive and for my highest good if I wish to have the life I want to live.

Reflections:

What I Know for Sure
If I change nothing, nothing will ever change

As I continue to grow and unfold, I know that a part of me needs to die, so that a higher spiritual part can wake up. Today, I die to the human. No longer do I panic or react. Instead I realize the human self with its patterns are dying, and I am now releasing from all that no longer serves me.

Reflections:

What I Know for Sure
If I change nothing, nothing will ever change

I must walk back into my disturbing past and call my spirit back from the painful places it was sent. I release myself from all illusions. I forgive myself and I forgive anyone who might have harmed me, real or imagined.

Reflections:

SEPTEMBER

What I Know for Sure
If I change nothing, nothing will ever change

As long as I hold the impression that someone is doing something to me, or something is happening to me, I am creating illusions that hold me hostage. What I know for sure; I must open myself to Divine Order to experience meaning, miracles, and spontaneous intuition in my life and affairs.

Reflections:

What I Know for Sure
If I change nothing, nothing will ever change

There are only two laws; man's laws and spiritual laws. I know for sure that I must unplug from the sequence of man's world and human events and live life on a much larger scale.

I open myself to Divine Sequencing.

Reflections:

What I Know for Sure
If I change nothing, nothing will ever change

I must stay humble and modest and focus on my spiritual development. I do not allow myself to be pulled into the economy, money, or concerns of this or that. What I know for sure is the adversary is attempting to make people worry and lose their focus. I am mindful.

Reflections:

What I Know for Sure
If I change nothing, nothing will ever change

I've been good to people in my life and they have been good to me. Spiritual maturity allows each to create their own space to grown, to nurture, to think, and to create. It's wonderful and each person should be allowed to have their quiet time, private time, and own space too. I know this for sure because it's our nature.

Reflections:

What I Know for Sure
If I change nothing, nothing will ever change

I must not lose myself in people. Because I place myself into a cause or a concern, I must not lose myself. What I know for sure; I must step back and view the drama like I'm watching a staged play. I remain seated in the audience, watching. I remain free from their story.

Reflections:

What I Know for Sure
If I change nothing, nothing will ever change

I must never lose myself in another, yet it is good to lose myself in the Divine. I must not try to blend their journey with mine. What I know for sure; I cannot live my life for others.

Reflections:

What I Know for Sure
If I change nothing, nothing will ever change

If there's ever a time to understand God on this planet, the time is NOW. Down the road, it's coming... we will not have the opportunity to learn about God, because someone else will be introduced. Most people will say, worship this or that God, because that God knows the most. What I know for sure; I must discern between what is authentic and what is artificial intelligence.

Reflections:

September 8   What I Know for Sure

What I Know for Sure
If I change nothing, nothing will ever change

If I pray in advance, then no one needs to tell me how to pray or who to pray to. It is better for me to know God and have a relationship with myself and the God of my own understanding. I draw near to God and know that God will draw near to me.

Reflections:

What I Know for Sure
If I change nothing, nothing will ever change

I must remain spiritually discerning, so I am not deliberately fooled by the adversary or negative thoughts, gossip, hearsay, and piercing arrows of poison. I have a choice. I will not be deceived or misled. I must always trust the still small voice within.

Reflections:

What I Know for Sure
If I change nothing, nothing will ever change

Distractions abound to take me off my course of Divine Right Action and Divine Right Thinking. Distractions are being made to get me to look over here, look over there, like I have no choice. I always have a choice to discern.

Reflections:

What I Know for Sure
If I change nothing, nothing will ever change

In the future sometime, drones, the size of insects, can listen in to our conversations and know where we are. This behavior controls the population. It's not just this country, it's the whole world. They want us to pray to this robotic being. People will be misled, looking God-like… This is destroying man-kind, so the adversary can steal all the souls. What I know for sure is that our job is to be spiritually awake and discerning.

Reflections:

What I Know for Sure
If I change nothing, nothing will ever change

I am not without Power. God is here. I must constantly pray and know that I am covered by this sacred blanket of God.

Reflections:

What I Know for Sure
If I change nothing, nothing will ever change

I recognize that I no longer have to fight battles. I no longer have to feel the need to belong. When I feel the need to belong, this may create within me a false persona of acting out and engaging in unhealthy behaviors.

Reflections:

What I Know for Sure
If I change nothing, nothing will ever change

Needing to belong makes people engage in unhealthy actions. Some people are searching for something, and when they go out into the world and find it, they don't have to search anymore. Many do not know what they're searching for. They are empty, trying to fill up. It doesn't work. They continue searching and looking and traveling.

What I know for sure; it is within.

Reflections:

What I Know for Sure
If I change nothing, nothing will ever change

On Perseverance: I know that I am being asked again to delve down far into the deepest need of my nature and tap into the most profound of resources for the molding of my character.

When I tap into myself, I see the need for perseverance, patience, and a clear path of conduct. I must be patient, and align self with my Higher Self.

Reflections:

September 16 — What I Know for Sure

What I Know for Sure
If I change nothing, nothing will ever change

Spiritual unions must both be timely and provide for both partners for a bond to be authentic. Devotion to a cause calls for perseverance and patience. This I know for sure.

Reflections:

What I Know for Sure
If I change nothing, nothing will ever change

Without using ears to hear, eyes to see, I fail to take advantage of the moment. Sometimes caution is needed. When hasty or ill-timed action occurs, life force can leak out, do not grieve.

I know that it has survived its time.

Everything has a beginning, middle, and end. I must not draw back when in deep water. I know for sure that I must become a swimmer and dive deeper.

Reflections:

September 18 — What I Know for Sure

What I Know for Sure
If I change nothing, nothing will ever change

Setbacks which I experienced were my teachers, allies, and guides. I smile at this with good humor, I show perseverance, and I don't give up. What I know for sure; this is a time to restore harmony and to restore balance.

Reflections:

What I Know for Sure
If I change nothing, nothing will ever change

On Relationship to Self: I must understand myself more. I must continue to work on me. Most persons do not understand themselves. I must be mindful that some things must manifest before progress.

Reflections:

September 20 — What I Know for Sure

What I Know for Sure
If I change nothing, nothing will ever change

On Patience: I must not persist in attempting to work my will. The seed of the new is present in the shell of the old. I am open and patient. I wait creatively and watch.

Reflections:

What I Know for Sure
If I change nothing, nothing will ever change

When I am dealing with constraints, I know that I must stand still and watch. Standing still represents the obstacles that I create as well as the obstacles I encounter, and both are difficult to handle. I don't take this world personally. I have learned to work with the shadow and examine what is in my nature that seems to attract hardship into my life. What I know for sure is that I now can look at this with a smile and know that everything is in Divine Order.

Reflections:

September 22 What I Know for Sure

What I Know for Sure
If I change nothing, nothing will ever change

I know the difference between a gut feeling and an inner knowing: Inner Knowing is knowledge from a strong relationship with God/ it is more than a hunch, and a gut feeling. Knowing without any shadow of a doubt, is enlightenment, inner knowing. With this, comes the serenity, that I've always searched for. I am on my quest.

Reflections:

What I Know for Sure
If I change nothing, nothing will ever change

The biggest obstacle I'm overcoming is staying out of my own way. I learn to let the will of heaven flow through me which puts me among spiritual warriors.

Reflections:

What I Know for Sure
If I change nothing, nothing will ever change

I forgive myself and I forgive you totally and unconditionally. I forgive your actions towards me. I know that your actions have made me stronger. I now know that through the healing power of forgiveness, I am growing spiritually, physically, mentally, and financially. I know that by forgiving you I am loving, caring, giving, successful, and prosperous.

Reflections:

What I Know for Sure
If I change nothing, nothing will ever change

Communication starts with being honest with yourself and understanding your thoughts, behaviors, and past experiences. Without this persistent and painstaking effort to do so, clear and honest communication often results in a severe retardation of family structures and values and a collapse in human relationships.

Reflections:

September 26 What I Know for Sure

What I Know for Sure
If I change nothing, nothing will ever change

Every experience has a cycle for everyone and everything has a beginning, and an end, and this is followed by a new beginning. I'm cycling out of one aspect of how I lived with community and entering a new beginning. I commit to change.

Reflections: What are you willing to commit to?

What I Know for Sure
If I change nothing, nothing will ever change

When life is tough and chaotic, I must connect with the wholeness of the sacred to find total peace. I must give peace, and I must share peace with others.

Reflections:

What I Know for Sure
If I change nothing, nothing will ever change

We are at the pause button on the earth plane.

When the pause button is released, then we will be facing tough, anxious, and scary times in our lives. It will be a difficult situation. Our life line will be with God, and we must remember to hang on to our life line. Spirit will awaken anyone who asks for it. What I know for sure; Spirit will give me wisdom and understanding.

Reflections:

What I Know for Sure
If I change nothing, nothing will ever change

On Emotions: I must not be controlled by emotions. We all fall short. I refuse to allow what happens to others take control, emotionally. I now align myself with good and know that God is the living waters.

Reflections:

September 30 — What I Know for Sure

What I Know for Sure
If I change nothing, nothing will ever change

On Emotions: I have emotions, but I am not my emotions. And I can control my emotions. Those who control their emotions rise to create important things, and those who do not control their emotions, develop leaks in the brain. Emotions are ours to control.

Reflections:

What I Know for Sure

OCTOBER

What I Know for Sure
If I change nothing, nothing will ever change

On Discernment: I must not go outside of self to find out about discernment. I am learning discernment. It takes a little time to recognize immediately when assessing an agreement, a product, a person, a project, or whatever it is. I do not go outside to ask for discernment. I will know in the moment when I am awake to intuition and consciousness.

Reflections:

October 2 — What I Know for Sure

What I Know for Sure
If I change nothing, nothing will ever change

Every person or experience I encounter is a learning experience, if I approach life with curiosity and openness for expansion of myself.

Reflections:

What I Know for Sure
If I change nothing, nothing will ever change

On Discernment: The more proof I have, the more evidence that I have, the closer I come to possess and achieve positive end results. During this time, I meditate and achieve wisdom and gain direction. I now have the clues needed to defeat anything negative, including the enemy, the adversary, or negative thoughts.

Reflections:

October 4 — What I Know for Sure

What I Know for Sure
If I change nothing, nothing will ever change

On Disruption: I may have a disruption happening in my life. It might be going on right now! Plans go left, instead of right. I know there will be disruptions in my life. I also know for sure that there is a light at the end of the tunnel. Prosperity will come from the disruption. I keep the faith.

Reflections:

What I Know for Sure
If I change nothing, nothing will ever change

Communication is connecting with Spirit and listening. When I listen, I am feeling universal love, trust, and forward movement with the direction that Spirit is giving me. I am listening, because the results I experience become positive. I do not give up. Even if I'm knocked down by the challenge or the enemy, I get right back up, and I get back on track. I am taking the challenge out of the challenge. I embrace the situation so that it does not fight against my inner peace.

Reflections:

What I Know for Sure
If I change nothing, nothing will ever change

Challenges are obstacles that can be overcome. We always learn from the experience or it is repeated.

Learn from the same experience twice and you say, "You know what, I think I got it now".

Reflections:

What I Know for Sure
If I change nothing, nothing will ever change

If the results of all my challenges become positive, and everything seems to be peaceful within, without, and around me, I have reached success.

Reflections:

What I Know for Sure
If I change nothing, nothing will ever change

When I ask Spirit to walk with me and reside in me, I know for sure that I am being led to the secret peace I am intimately seeking. Universal Oneness is the teacher. I will be spoken to and it will be disclosed to me what is to come, and I will be given Truth. I know for sure that I must always walk in the Spirit, filled with the Spirit and I will find the Peace that I am seeking, which is always seeking me.

Reflections:

What I Know for Sure
If I change nothing, nothing will ever change

Sometimes I enter relationships, and my bond becomes a real one. I have devotion, just as one might have devotion to a cause, as to an idea, I have devotion to conduct. I counseled, I have perseverance, but at times, I need patience.

Reflections: What do you need more of in your life today?

What I Know for Sure
If I change nothing, nothing will ever change

Loving someone is having the right thoughts about them. Loving someone is thinking positive about them, projecting and knowing the best for that person, doing the best to help them achieve their goals, desires, and dreams, as well as caring for that person.

Reflections:

What I Know for Sure
If I change nothing, nothing will ever change

In the game of life, my dedication, devotion and persistence to listening to my inner voice, believing it to be my truth and taking action, allows me to move through life with ease in a state of grace.

Reflections:

October 12 — What I Know for Sure

What I Know for Sure
If I change nothing, nothing will ever change

People have regrets about choices they made and find it difficult to forgive themselves. There is never a wrong choice. I choose according to what I want to learn now. I can always choose a new course.

Reflections:

What I Know for Sure
If I change nothing, nothing will ever change

People inherently know within that they've made choices that are not in their highest or best interest. They are resistant to change, primarily because of the energy they've expended.

Reflections:

What I Know for Sure
If I change nothing, nothing will ever change

Many relationships never end because people are afraid of letting go or being alone on a Saturday night.

If I made unhealthy choices, it does not mean I should stay involved in insanity. I must recognize when it is time to move on for the wellbeing of all involved. I must free us from captivity.

Reflections:

What I Know for Sure
If I change nothing, nothing will ever change

My assignment is unique; therefore, my responsibility is to look to my internal compass and heart for the answer I seek, as others cannot know my path.

Reflections:

October 16   What I Know for Sure

What I Know for Sure
If I change nothing, nothing will ever change

When I stay positive and think right thoughts, abundance occurs in my life.

Reflections:

What I Know for Sure
If I change nothing, nothing will ever change

Distractions can be pleasingly enticing and lead me astray. I must remain aware and awake, choosing wisely. My choices determine the outcome.

Reflections:

October 18 What I Know for Sure

What I Know for Sure
If I change nothing, nothing will ever change

While I don't always recognize why I feel depressed or in despair, the sooner I address my negative thoughts, and transform them, I am able to rise to greater heights. Thoughts create things.

Reflections:

What I Know for Sure
If I change nothing, nothing will ever change

I am stronger than I realize, and I have the strength to handle anything which comes my way with compassion, kindness, and forgiveness, when I am in alignment with Spirit.

Reflections:

What I Know for Sure
If I change nothing, nothing will ever change

When I recognize my loved one's pain, my role is to be openhearted, loving and supportive while inquiring gently and directly, allowing my love to bring up their strength, truth and courage to help lift heavy burdens they are carrying.

As difficult as it to observe their pain, I support them without interference.

Reflections:

What I Know for Sure
If I change nothing, nothing will ever change

The more I live my life in alignment with the Divine, the more peace, love, and harmony I experience, even as challenges arise. How I approach any challenge determines the ease with which it is resolved. My thoughts and reactions create my reality. It is best to go within instead of without to obtain the answers.

Reflections:

October 22 — What I Know for Sure

What I Know for Sure
If I change nothing, nothing will ever change

When life presents opportunity for change and I resist, roadblocks occur. If I surrender the outcome to God and open myself with wonder, new opportunities appear with ease. When I surrender and ask for help, answers come effortlessly.

Reflections:

What I Know for Sure
If I change nothing, nothing will ever change

If I feel alone, lost and isolated, it maybe I am experiencing a major growth spurt on my personal quest. Taking time alone to explore is necessary for integration. I give myself permission to explore my feelings in my own time.

Reflections:

What I Know for Sure
If I change nothing, nothing will ever change

The biggest obstacle that I am overcoming is staying out of my own way.

I learn to let the will of heaven flow. This flow places me among spiritual warriors.

My energy is like a sword. I use it to cut away the dead, what I no longer need.

With warrior knowledge comes wisdom that the universe will have the first move, and patience will be my virtue. I know for sure that the reward of patience is patience. I continue to look within, delving into the foundation of my life itself and there at the core of my depth, I will meet the deepest need of my nature and tap into my most profound resources; the molding of my character.

Reflections:

What I Know for Sure
If I change nothing, nothing will ever change

Upon hearing negative comments about self, my work, my product, or about healings, I do not fall into the trap of believing negative comments. I practice discernment carefully and consistently. I realize the enemy is trying to derail me. When this happens, it tells me that I am getting closer to reaching success, otherwise, why is the enemy trying to derail me? I talk to God, I ask God to calmly guide my thoughts. I do not let fear paralyze me. I pray, "Dear God, connect with me right now, and show me discernment, so that my antenna goes directly to you."

Reflections:

What I Know for Sure
If I change nothing, nothing will ever change

With the dawn of each day, just as the sun rises, so do I with thanks and gratitude for all the possibilities which await me. Greet each day with an eagerness to expand.

Reflections:

What I Know for Sure
If I change nothing, nothing will ever change

All the wisdom I need to advance myself was gifted by God when I entered this lifetime. Prayer, meditation and trust of self is all I need. No one knows better than me. I make time to listen.

Reflections:

October 28 — What I Know for Sure

What I Know for Sure
If I change nothing, nothing will ever change

I dated and married abusive partners always. Seeing my patterns is shocking and hard for me to swallow. Choosing to date partners who don't abuse me today is frightening and a challenge. I must ask myself, am I willing to take the risk of dating healthy people?

Reflections:

What I Know for Sure
If I change nothing, nothing will ever change

Until I recognize and release the old patterns of allowing men to abuse me, I set the course of abuse in my children lives. I must break negative abusive patterns and replace them with conscious loving men who exhibit healthy behaviors.

Reflections:

What I Know for Sure
If I change nothing, nothing will ever change

Within the soul is the part and parcel of a meaningful life. I must nurture my inner self with discernment, wisdom, compassion, faith, love, and hope; this I know for sure.

Reflections:

What I Know for Sure
If I change nothing, nothing will ever change

If I keep running from and running away, I rob myself of opportunities to learn, grow, or change. When I run, my backpack weighs me down, and my bones are heavy bearing the flight, fright, and fight within my body. If I do nothing, I'll continue to remain homeless, hopeless, and hapless.

Reflections:

What I Know for Sure

NOVEMBER

What I Know for Sure
If I change nothing, nothing will ever change

Helping others is like helping myself. We are here to learn the same lessons. We learn through our own stories. Different stories same lesson. Therefore, helping another often shows up so I can help myself. The words I share with another are for me as well.

Reflections:

What I Know for Sure
If I change nothing, nothing will ever change

People show up in our lives seeking help from us, but it often leads to helping ourselves and we don't always recognize it. When we remain open to understanding that those we interact with are teachers in their own way we grow. If we fail to recognize, we miss valuable opportunities for growth.

Reflections:

What I Know for Sure
If I change nothing, nothing will ever change

When I deny, hide, or bury my gifts I am cheating myself and others' who would benefit with my loving assistance. It is time to discover, uncover, and recover my gifts.

Reflections:

What I Know for Sure
If I change nothing, nothing will ever change

People pleasing at my own expense leads to feeling void and unfulfilled. When I do things that I don't want to do, I'm often trying to please others. But upon investigation I find learned negative behavior patterns from my past infringing upon my present which bind me to the patterns I want so desperately to change.

Reflections:

What I Know for Sure
If I change nothing, nothing will ever change

I realized that based on personal experiences, without making changes, you can visit a place or person and see them stuck in their story, stuck in the loop, stuck in the spokes of the wheel of their life, repeating pattern after pattern after pattern. Looking back over the panorama of my life, I didn't realize until I took a leap of faith to change. Wow! How that leap afforded me opportunities for growth and expansion and a wider vision of a power greater than myself that I now come to believe in.

Reflections:

What I Know for Sure
If I change nothing, nothing will ever change

We each have a plan this lifetime. My responsibility is to navigate successfully my soul's growth.

Reflections:

What I Know for Sure
If I change nothing, nothing will ever change

Sometimes the greatest gifts appear in the most unexpected ways. Our angels are always watching over and guiding us to our greatest good.

Reflections:

November 8   What I Know for Sure

What I Know for Sure
If I change nothing, nothing will ever change

Stretching my mind is as important as stretching my body. The result is greater fluidity, flexibility, focus and freedom. I stretch to a greater capacity, expanding my boundaries, expanding my life.

Reflections:

What I Know for Sure
If I change nothing, nothing will ever change

What I know for sure is when I deny myself the freedom of choice I lose my voice. Today I choose me! I am empowered! I am heard!

Reflections:

What I Know for Sure
If I change nothing, nothing will ever change

My spiritual expansiveness comes from a desire within, a willingness and faith to go deeper into self. I recognize the wisdom to navigate life has been provided by God.

Reflections:

What I Know for Sure
If I change nothing, nothing will ever change

I am the driver of my vehicle. I must care for it and fuel it mentally, emotionally and spiritually, as well as physically to function well.

Reflections:

November 12   What I Know for Sure

What I Know for Sure
If I change nothing, nothing will ever change

As a mother I must remember despite my thoughts and feelings about my child's undertakings in the world, I am best suited by allowing them to discover the ups and downs of life on their own. I will always be available to lift them up after a fall.

Reflections:

What I Know for Sure
If I change nothing, nothing will ever change

Insidious distractions abound instantly and constantly. People's eyes are on the economy and the fighting happening in the world. These distractions pulled them away from their true purpose of what they can do right now. We must stay focused and stay on course.

Reflections:

November 14   What I Know for Sure

What I Know for Sure
If I change nothing, nothing will ever change

To be who I truly am, I must overcome the fears of my own success and step fearlessly into the life I choose to live.

Reflections:

What I Know for Sure
If I change nothing, nothing will ever change

When I hear a whisper in my ear or a nudge to do something, I pay attention to the signs, they often show up when you least expect them, and I experience unexpected good in my life.

Reflections:

What I Know for Sure
If I change nothing, nothing will ever change

There's something about outgrowing things, realizing it is time to move on. People and events are in our lives for a reason and I refuse to be attached to people, places, or things.

Reflections:

What I Know for Sure
If I change nothing, nothing will ever change

I follow the road of my heart. The road of the heart is the Divine road that connects with Good Orderly Direction.

Reflections:

What I Know for Sure
If I change nothing, nothing will ever change

I know longer allow others to impose their negativity into my energy field. I know that I must remain in alignment with my own energy. I welcome it. I greet it. I own it. I cultivate oneness. I dissolve any negativity that is going on in my own energy field.

Reflections:

What I Know for Sure
If I change nothing, nothing will ever change

Today I recognize my strength, courage and power. By owning all parts of myself and knowing the truth of the Creator's love and desire of good for me, I am able to propel myself forward with confidence knowing I am supported.

Reflections:

What I Know for Sure
If I change nothing, nothing will ever change

I know how to be still. I know who God is. I know what Serenity is.

Reflections:

What I Know for Sure
If I change nothing, nothing will ever change

When I write what I am thankful and grateful for each day including the smallest things, it reminds me of the good in my life, and the universe continues to send me good.

Reflections:

What I Know for Sure
If I change nothing, nothing will ever change

I began separating paths with others, there was a peeling away and a discarding. I've always been a seeker, even in my younger days. I wasn't quite sure, but I wanted a new, fresh life, and no longer the old. I became a spiritual follower, and my conquest is still with me and is strong to this day. I seek change constantly.

Reflections:

What I Know for Sure
If I change nothing, nothing will ever change

People are extremely difficult, yet we cannot live without them. Everyone wants comfort and strives for it; the ability to go where they want to go and do what they want to do and live the way they want to live. People want comfort.

I ask myself, what is it that I'm striving for? What is it that I'm working for? It must be more than comfortability. People work hard for comfort and when they get it, they are not comfortable.

Reflections:

November 24   What I Know for Sure

What I Know for Sure
If I change nothing, nothing will ever change

Being comfortable in my skin, being comfortable with Spirit, I am at peace. If I do not connect with the Creator of the Universe, I will always be seeking hard to attain comfort.

I know that I've worked hard for this in my life and I am connecting and receiving comfort from God.

Reflections:

What I Know for Sure
If I change nothing, nothing will ever change

The secret place of all secret places, I know that everyone wants peace, not material things, not happiness.

I know for sure it is within themselves; peace…that passes all understanding.

Reflections:

November 26 What I Know for Sure

What I Know for Sure
If I change nothing, nothing will ever change

The light within me can never be extinguished. When I notice my light becoming dim, I take immediate action. I move out of the shadows and claim my power.

What do I need to address?

Reflections:

What I Know for Sure
If I change nothing, nothing will ever change

My human self is not a gift, I am an achievement. I am a painfully past reality of my triumphs over battles, my triumphs over obstacles, triumphs over negative people, negative gossip, negative experiences, and ogres, real or imagine. The attainment of my best and highest good is a never-ending process. It is never about my reputation to the world, but what I truly am within myself. My ultimate essential goal is to achieve self-mastery. This I know for sure!

Reflections:

What I Know for Sure
If I change nothing, nothing will ever change

Who am I with and how do I feel when I'm with them?

Do I say no when I don't want to be there?

Do I repeat damaging patterns like?

- Staying in an unhappy marriage
- Convincing myself that nothing is wrong
- Arguing how right I am, and how others are wrong
- Controlling
- Being a clown
- Lying about a situation or an event

Do I repeat the above patterns to please my partner, or other people?

If I Change Nothing, Nothing Will Ever Change.

Reflections:

What I Know for Sure
If I change nothing, nothing will ever change

What Lies am I telling myself?

- I'm going to keep this job until my children graduate from H. S. or College
- I'm going to stay in this relationship for five years
- This is not my guy/girl, but I am staying in this relationship to learn my lesson

How is this serving me?

Where is my integrity?

Reflections:

November 30 What I Know for Sure

What I Know for Sure
If I change nothing, nothing will ever change

Excuses are reason for stagnation, leading to procrastination. Using _____ is an excuse to not change a circumstance in my life that I want to change.

Reflections:

What I Know for Sure

DECEMBER

What I Know for Sure
If I change nothing, nothing will ever change

Low self-esteem was my best friend. I told lies to everyone. I wanted attention and praise. I didn't know how to just be… me…my lies hurt many. I knew I wanted friends, so I decided to act better. I became humble, made amends to those I had hurt, and changes occurred to set me free. I still have work to do, but I know that if I change nothing, nothing will ever change.

Reflections:

December 2   What I Know for Sure

What I Know for Sure
If I change nothing, nothing will ever change

We are all on the same ride…back home.

Follow your heart.

Reflections:

What I Know for Sure
If I change nothing, nothing will ever change

Throughout life people called me selfish. Through the process of deep disclosure and intimate self-examination, I found self-care was in my best interest. Selflessly I remain devoted to my mission. No one knows what I need, better than me. My purpose is to thrive not merely survive.

Reflections:

December 4   What I Know for Sure

What I Know for Sure
If I change nothing, nothing will ever change

I blamed others for my deficiencies. I blamed my parents for how my life was. What I failed to see was that no matter what they did or didn't do, my life was my responsibility. Now as an adult, I'm faced with the truth that if I do not make changes and stop blaming, then nothing in my life will ever change. When I blame others for where I am in life, instead of taking responsibility for myself, I cut myself off from the sunlight of the Spirit and suffer Infinite loss. I choose to grow up.

What are you willing to give up creating change in your life?

Reflections:

What I Know for Sure
If I change nothing, nothing will ever change

Living this life in harmony is extremely difficult during these last days on earth because everything is thrown at me. It feels like I am going in circles, it feels like I did this before and I sometimes question myself, "why are you doing that again?" The adversary is trying to turn things around. It is happening to many people right now. It feels like being picked on or bullied. Many are turning to a monetary advantage at this time and forget about their eternal advantage. I know for sure that I trust the Creator. I am a true child of light and I have faith.

Reflections:

What I Know for Sure
If I change nothing, nothing will ever change

After attending a workshop or spiritual retreat I feel confident. I must remain conscious of people testing me, trying to lure me back into old ways, patterns, and behaviors. My real work begins when the workshop is over!

It requires an inner willingness to prompt a deep commitment to bring forth the kind of lasting change that I want in my life now.

Reflections:

What I Know for Sure
If I change nothing, nothing will ever change

People are forever trying to change others. I make changes within myself, without expecting others to change. I lead by demonstration in my life and those who like what they see, can benefit from my changes.

Reflections:

December 8 — What I Know for Sure

What I Know for Sure
If I change nothing, nothing will ever change

When people in my life try to poison me with negative thoughts, actions and words, it is my spiritual responsibility to rise above negative innuendo, remaining faithful and unperturbed. I remember that the thoughts I think weave the fabric of my life.

Reflections:

What I Know for Sure
If I change nothing, nothing will ever change

My secret to success is faith in the One Divine Creative Mind recognizing I can have, be, or do anything I want when I stand in an unmovable, unshakable, foundation and know that anything I declare is obtainable.

Reflections:

December 10   What I Know for Sure

What I Know for Sure
If I change nothing, nothing will ever change

What is rightfully mine in the eyes of God no one can take from me including my strength, courage and dignity as well as any material things I desire and choose to have?

Reflections:

What I Know for Sure
If I change nothing, nothing will ever change

My gifts are treasures waiting for me to uncover. No one else can do the work but me. I am the way to discovery through dedicated work and perseverance.

Reflections:

December 12   What I Know for Sure

What I Know for Sure
If I change nothing, nothing will ever change

Each day I get to create my own reality and paint a new picture. I approach each day like a blank canvas.

Reflections:

What I Know for Sure
If I change nothing, nothing will ever change

The lies I tell myself, the lies I tell others only hurt me. I am unable to form honest relationships based on lies.

Lies, Lies, Lies!!!

If I continue to lie nothing will ever change!

My priority is to stop lying and to be honest. Then, I may be able to project truth to myself and others.

Reflections: What are you lying about? Time to get real.

December 14   What I Know for Sure

What I Know for Sure
If I change nothing, nothing will ever change

Often the work that must be done is not easy or pleasant, but it reaps the greatest rewards. What will it cost me if I do not do my spiritual work?

Reflections:

What I Know for Sure
If I change nothing, nothing will ever change

Removing myself from others drama and repeat stories is vital for my health and wellbeing. It is absolutely necessary for me to live from my own experiences.

Reflections:

December 16 What I Know for Sure

What I Know for Sure
If I change nothing, nothing will ever change

Transformational transcendence helps me to understand myself, my relationship to life, and my oneness with God.

Reflections:

What I Know for Sure
If I change nothing, nothing will ever change

I am here to wake myself up from the illusions and lies held in my mind and told to me by others. If they choose not to wake up, it is not my concern. I am only responsible for shaking myself from the sleep that held me hostage and in captivity.

Reflections:

December 18 What I Know for Sure

What I Know for Sure
If I change nothing, nothing will ever change

What I know for sure: I find joy in life's simple pleasures: sunrises and sunsets.

Reflections:

What I Know for Sure
If I change nothing, nothing will ever change

When someone dear to my heart is preparing to cross over, I gently allow them to exit this earth with love and no attachments, realizing that there is no death, only a continual renewal of life. I remain in love and gratitude for this beautiful being having touched my life. Their essential being is eternal, and I bless them as their journey continues.

Reflections:

What I Know for Sure
If I change nothing, nothing will ever change

Lovers who meet during low periods in their life, and cling to one another for security can only invite a hostage situation which may lead to selfish survival instead of emotional and spiritual growth. One certainly can miss the signs along the highway of life in a sacred manner when it is time to need self. Always remain authentic by cleaning up the wreckage of one's past before engaging in relationships.

Reflections:

What I Know for Sure
If I change nothing, nothing will ever change

Now is the time to fully know myself and share my light to the world.

Reflections:

December 22 — What I Know for Sure

What I Know for Sure
If I change nothing, nothing will ever change

I am being led. I am hearing with my heart. I hear God speak to my heart in the silence.

Reflections:

Ayin M. Adams, Ph.D. / Ciaara K. Carlsen   **December 23**

What I Know for Sure
If I change nothing, nothing will ever change

A picture truly is worth a thousand words… paint your own masterpiece.

Reflections:

What I Know for Sure
If I change nothing, nothing will ever change

What I know for sure: every experience I have in my life happens for a reason, though I may not see it now. Looking back, it's the best thing that could have happened for me.

Reflections:

What I Know for Sure
If I change nothing, nothing will ever change

Whatever my purpose, it is my gift to share with the world. I know why I am on the planet. I know what to do. I am empowered by universal intuitive language. I hear the still small voice, and I know for sure I rise.

Reflections:

December 26   What I Know for Sure

What I Know for Sure
If I change nothing, nothing will ever change

I am unique as a snowflake. There is only one like me. I am on my pilgrimage and therefore I should stay true to my path without competing or comparing myself with others. Comparing myself to others is not to my advantage. I must compare myself to myself.

I am better than I was yesterday, last week, last month, and definitely one year ago.

Reflections:

What I Know for Sure
If I change nothing, nothing will ever change

Often, I forget that we are humans, here to play the game of life together. How we play depends on our consciousness and the realization we all came from one light; therefore, we are more alike than different. When I look for similarities in those around me I can be kinder, more compassionate, and understanding, remembering earth school is a place where we learn and grow before returning home.

Reflections:

December 28 What I Know for Sure

What I Know for Sure
If I change nothing, nothing will ever change

Many people are unconscious thinking people, or habitual negative thinkers, meaning their thought is purely reactive. In other words, many assume their thought is produced by circumstances that they meet, and they react.

Our upsets, fears, worries, and disappointments are all caused by the conditions about which we are upset. This is not true at all, it seems this way. What I know for sure, we must stop the way we have always conditioned ourselves to think and begin to think from a spiritual mind-set.

Reflections: What are some ways of thinking that you must change?

What I Know for Sure
If I change nothing, nothing will ever change

Whatever problems a person may have, their problems are thinking. They think illogical thought, confused thought, and negative thought. We try to fight our way through problems, to beg or cheat our way through, but it's only when we THINK our way through that we begin to find answers.

In other words, when we meditate and pray our way through problems, this becomes thought on the highest perspective. It becomes high level thinking, and transcendental thinking.

Reflections: What thoughts are you thinking?

December 30   What I Know for Sure

What I Know for Sure
If I change nothing, nothing will ever change

Change is just a decision away, choose your life Now! When I get stuck and go into a place of depression, I feel out of alignment, things are not right.

When I sense uncomfortable noise in my body, or static, it persists until I stop and say to myself, "Tomorrow is a new day."

Reflections:

What I Know for Sure
If I change nothing, nothing will ever change

What I know for sure: if I choose stagnation, I die.

Reflections:

About the Authors

Ayin Adams, Msc.D., D.D., Spiritual Director and a Holistic teacher of self-development and consciousness. Adams utilizes her gift of words to heal and educate. Adams is the author of more than eight books. Adams documents our passage in time using her writings and tonality of voice to help one break out of the current constraints and fragmentation of daily habitual life. She assists and facilitates individuals to co-create their futures, especially as many of the established structures of society may be falling away. Adams lives with the intention of suiting up, showing up, and following through. Adams embraces a firm belief that everything is in Divine Order.

Ciaara K. Carlsen is a Metaphysical Practitioner. She studies Science of Mind principles and the Kabalarian Philosophy, aimed at a balance of body, mind, and spirit which strengthens the mind and enhances positive qualities. Ciaara achieves dramatic results working with clients. This is her first book born out of personal growth and development.

www.ingramcontent.com/pod-product-compliance
Lightning Source LLC
Chambersburg PA
CBHW071647160426
43195CB00012B/1387